MADISON CENTRAL SCHOOL

ESEA TITLE I I
SPECIAL PURPOSE
INCENTIVE GRANT

People of Destiny

A Humanities Series

There comes a time,
we know not when,
that marks
the destiny of men.

Joseph Addison Alexander

People of Destiny

DOUGLAS MacARTHUR

By Norman Richards

*For their cooperation in reviewing this manuscript
the editors wish to express their appreciation
to Major General Courtney Whitney, former personal
Aide to General of the Army Douglas MacArthur and
to Colonel Laurence Eliot Bunker, former personal
Aide to General of the Army Douglas MacArthur*

CHILDRENS PRESS, CHICAGO

*The editors wish to express
their appreciation to Mr. Meyer Goldberg,
who created the series and inspired
the publication of* People of Destiny.

Cover and body design: John Hollis

Project editor: Joan Downing

Editorial assistant: Gerri Stoller

*Illustrations: Bob Brunton, Nita Engle —
Hollis Associates*

Research editor: Robert Hendrickson

*Photographs: From the files of Wide
World Photos, Inc.*

Typesetting: Black Dot, Inc.

Printing: The Regensteiner Corporation

Quotations on pages 24, 33, 39, 40, 45, 62, 66, and 72 from Reminiscences, by General of the Army Douglas MacArthur. McGraw-Hill Book Co., New York, 1964. Used by permission of McGraw-Hill Book Company.
Quotations on pages 50 and 68-69 from Douglas MacArthur, by Alfred Steinberg. G.P. Putnam's Sons, New York, 1961.
Quotations on pages 16, 32, and 56 from Front Line General; Douglas MacArthur, by Jules Archer. Julian Messner, New York, 1963.

Contents

Hero of Controversy

A chill wind blew dark storm clouds over the coast of Japan on the afternoon of April 11, 1951. Gusts swirled around the corners of a tall, impressive building in Tokyo —the American Embassy, residence and personal headquarters of General of the Army Douglas Mac-Arthur. As Supreme Commander for Allied Powers he had ruled Japan for more than five years in austere, aloof fashion. The Japanese regarded the famed American war hero as an awesome figure, a leader of the conquering forces who had ruled a defeated nation with justice and mercy.

In the embassy dining room the erect seventy-one-year-old soldier and his wife were having lunch with some official guests. He was preparing to leave on a visit to Korea the following day. A conflict had been raging there for nearly a year between forces of the United Nations and the Communist armies of North Korea and China. As Supreme Commander of United Nations Forces in Korea, MacArthur had led the rescue of South Korea from invading Communists and had nearly achieved total victory before Red China intervened. Now the war seemed stalemated. The Communists didn't have the strength to win, but the United Nations armies, largely American and South Korean, were prevented from winning because MacArthur had orders from Washington prohibiting his forces from destroying the enemy's supply lines and bases inside Red China. Never one to shun controversy, MacArthur had protested angrily to government leaders and had made his views public.

Now the world-famous military leader sat finishing his coffee and telling his guests an amusing story. There was a message for Mrs. MacArthur, and she left the room. She returned a few minutes later with a shocked expression on her face. After waiting for the general to finish his story she leaned over him and whispered the startling news in a choked voice. His face remained impassive for a moment, then he squeezed her hand and said softly, "Well, Jeannie, I guess we're going home at last."

The news that Mrs. MacArthur had whispered startled the whole world. General Douglas MacArthur, the most successful military leader of the twentieth century, was being relieved of his command by the President of his country.

President Truman had issued a statement to the press: "With deep regret I have concluded that General of the Army Douglas MacArthur is unable to give his wholehearted support to the policies of the United States Government and of the United Nations. . . . I have, therefore, relieved General MacArthur of his commands and have designated Lieutenant General Matthew B. Ridgeway as his successor. . . . General MacArthur's place in history as one of our greatest commanders is fully established. The nation owes him a debt of gratitude for the distinguished and exceptional service which he has rendered his country. . . . I repeat my regret at the necessity for the action I feel compelled to take."

Newspapers all over the world carried the momentous news in bold headlines. Many readers were stunned and shocked; others were delighted. How could this have happened? Did it mean that the career of one of history's greatest military commanders was ending in sad disgrace?

Not at all. This world-shaking event was the climax of an explosive career that had been marked by a long series of controversies. And, true to form, Douglas MacArthur emerged from this one as a hero to millions of people and an arrogant egotist to his many detractors. People in all countries and all walks of life chose sides in the controversy, arguing that MacArthur was right or that he was wrong.

President Truman felt strongly that the Korean conflict must be limited to that area. He believed that the course MacArthur advocated—bombing Red Chinese bases and allowing anti-Communist Chinese to invade China from Formosa—would plunge the United States into a full-scale war with Red China. Concerned about the possibility of a global war, General Omar N. Bradley declared that MacArthur's proposals "would involve us in the wrong war, at the wrong place, at the wrong time, with the wrong enemy."

A lone United States marine stands bundled against the cold as he does sentry duty on a knoll somewhere in Korea in January, 1951. A few months later, in April, General of the Army Douglas MacArthur, Supreme Commander of United Nations Forces in Korea, was relieved of his command by President Harry S. Truman.

The President had ordered the Joint Chiefs of Staff to remind MacArthur of his directive forbidding MacArthur to make any more public statements about his views. But never in his long career had Douglas MacArthur remained silent when he felt he was right. He did not do so now. In a letter to Congressman Joseph W. Martin he criticized Truman's policies, adding, "We must win. There is no substitute for victory."

The controversy came to a head when Congressman Martin read the letter aloud on the floor of the House of Representatives in support of MacArthur's position. Truman decided he must act, since MacArthur had disobeyed his order to remain silent and had appealed directly to the American people. He read his fateful statement to the press at one o'clock in the morning on April 11, 1951.

A few days later, General and Mrs. MacArthur left their embassy quarters for the last time and embarked on the long journey home to America. Arthur, their thirteen-year-old son, was excited about the trip as he climbed into the limousine with his parents. He had been born in the Philippines and had spent his

Lights often blazed far into the night at General Douglas MacArthur's headquarters in Tokyo as he conferred with his aides during the many crises of the Korean conflict. Now, after making Japan their home and headquarters for more than five years, the MacArthurs were preparing to return to the United States.

young life in the Far East during World War II and the postwar occupation of Japan. He eagerly awaited his first look at his home country.

General MacArthur received the greatest tribute ever accorded a foreigner in the history of Japan. When he left, more than two million Japanese citizens lined the route to the airport where his plane awaited.

His reception was even greater in the United States. When he landed at Honolulu, it seemed as if everyone in the Hawaiian Islands had turned out to greet the last of America's great World War II heroes to return home. It was more of the same in San Francisco and Washington, where giant throngs greeted him wildly.

MacArthur was invited to address a joint session of Congress and responded by making one of the most eloquent speeches ever given before that body. In the address he defended his views on the war in Korea, declaring:

"Efforts have been made to distort my position. It has been said in effect that I was a warmonger. Nothing could be further from the truth.

"I know war as few other men now living know it, and nothing to me is more revolting. . . .

"But once war is forced upon us, there is no other alternative than to apply every available means to bring it to a swift end. War's very object is victory, not prolonged indecision. In war there is no substitute for victory. . . .

"I am now closing my fifty-two years of military service. When I joined the army, even before the turn of the century, it was the fulfillment of all my boyish hopes and dreams.

"The world has turned over many times since I took the oath on the plain at West Point, and the hopes and dreams have long since vanished. But I still remember the refrain of one of the most popular barrack ballads of that day which proclaimed most proudly that 'Old

"...War's very object is victory, not prolonged indecision. ...there is no substitute for victory...."

General MacArthur used these words as he addressed a joint session of Congress in Washington shortly after his return from the Far East. In the address he defended his views on the war in Korea.

soldiers never die, they just fade away.'

"And like the old soldier of that ballad, I now close my military career and just fade away—an old soldier who tried to do his duty as God gave him the light to see that duty. Goodbye."

Predictably, MacArthur's admirers were moved to tears by his dramatic farewell speech, and his detractors were annoyed. A newspaper columnist wrote, "If the American people have anything to say about our history books, it's obvious from their reverence for MacArthur that he's going to become one of our folk heroes along with Washington, Lee, and Grant."

Critics replied that "the melodramatic speech was typical of this egotist, who has always had a flair for the dramatic."

In New York, a short time after MacArthur's address to Congress, more than seven million people turned out to greet the MacArthurs with a ticker tape parade. The mayor presented the famed soldier with a special gold medal to express "the city's esteem and affection."

It was fitting that Douglas MacArthur should climax his long, colorful career with a swirling controversy, in the center of the world stage. In fact, he did not bow out of the public spotlight at all, but continued to reap honors and stir the fires of debate for several years afterward.

It seemed as if his destiny was to take part in crucial events throughout his life. From his early years through his long military career he was a man to be reckoned with—a giant who cast a tall shadow across the pages of his country's vivid history. He was destined to be loved, worshipped, feared, hated, and envied—but never ignored.

In New York, a short time after MacArthur's address to Congress, more than seven million people turned out to greet the MacArthurs with a ticker tape parade.

Listen!
O Listen!

It is not surprising that Douglas MacArthur chose a military life when his family background is considered. He was a descendent of fierce Scottish clansmen who formed a branch of the Campbell clan named MacArtair. They were among the earliest family groups in Scotland, as pointed out by the ancient adage: "There is nothing older, except the hills, MacArtair, and the devil."

The clan's battle cry was "Listen! O Listen!" and it referred to warriors listening for the rallying sound of bagpipes. It can be found in the ancient Scottish lyric:

"O the bags they are piping on banks of Loch Awe, And a voice on Cruachau calls the Lairds of Lochaw; 'MacArtair, Most High, where the wild myrtles glisten, Come, buckle your sword belt, and Listen! O Listen!'"

Douglas MacArthur's grandfather, Arthur MacArthur, came to America as a boy with his widowed mother in 1825. They settled in Massachusetts where the boy studied law and attended Wesleyan College. A few years after being admitted to the bar he packed his belongings and moved west with his wife and four-year-old son, also named Arthur.

America was expanding westward, and thousands of hardy pioneers were uprooting their

homes and traveling to new lands in wagons and canal boats. Lawyers were needed in the new communities being settled, and the young Scottish-born attorney decided to seek opportunity in the city of Milwaukee. He quickly established a reputation as a vigorous, able man of high principles and became very successful in his career. He became city attorney for Milwaukee, then a judicial circuit judge, and eventually an associate justice of the Supreme Court of the District of Columbia, where he served eighteen years before retiring.

But the old clan war cry "Listen! O Listen!" was deeply rooted in the family tradition, and it came back to haunt the imagination of the lawyer's young son, Arthur. When the Civil War broke out, Arthur was not yet sixteen, but he dreamed of entering military service.

"Dad," he said excitedly, "I'm going to volunteer."

"Aye, son, but not yet," his father replied. "I'll send you to military school for a year — and then, God be with you."

After an impatient year at military school, young Arthur was appointed a first lieutenant and adjutant of the Twenty-fourth Wisconsin Volunteer Infantry and went off to war. He distinguished himself in many battles and was decorated for gallantry in action. Finally, in the bloody battle of Missionary Ridge, he led the charge to the battle cry "On, Wisconsin!" with such bravery that he was awarded the Congressional Medal of Honor. He was wounded twice during the war and wound up as a temporary colonel at the tender age of nineteen.

Douglas MacArthur was a descendent of fierce Scottish clansmen who formed a branch of the Campbell clan named Mac-Artair. The clan's battle cry was "Listen! O Listen!" It referred to warriors listening for the rallying sound of bagpipes.

19

In November, 1863, Union troops were pinned down by intense Confederate fire at the foot of Missionary Ridge. Their orders were to capture the ridge, but their advance had been halted by the fierce storm of bullets and shells coming from the enemy positions on the slopes and crest.

Suddenly, in the smoke of battle, the flag of the Twenty-fourth Wisconsin Infantry Regiment advanced up the slope. It was carried by the color sergeant, who was accompanied by the color guard of two corporals. The adjutant, young Lieutenant Arthur MacArthur, led them as the flag was rushed straight at the Confederate lines in the thick of the fight.

The sergeant fell in the hail of bullets, and one of the corporals grabbed the colors. He was bayoneted a moment later. A shell burst on the group and killed the other corporal. Now Arthur MacArthur was alone as he grasped the flag and plunged forward in the midst of the enemy. He turned, and above the roar of the battle his clear voice sounded: "On, Wisconsin!"

The effect on the battered Union troops was electrifying. They surged up the slope in a fierce charge, overrunning the Confederates until they neared the top of the ridge. Then the determined enemy defenders rallied. The charge was halted with deadly fire. Men fell by the scores in the withering fusillade.

Then came that cry again: "On, Wisconsin!" Eyes turned to the crest and there, silhouetted against the sky, stood the young adjutant waving the colors. Again the charge was renewed and the Union troops fought and clawed their way to the top and to victory. The battle was over.

Arthur MacArthur collapsed as the division commander, General Philip Sheridan, approached to congratulate him. MacArthur's face was bloody and blackened with smoke, his clothes torn by bayonets.

"Take good care of this young man," General Sheridan said. "He has just won the Congressional Medal of Honor."

Arthur turned to the study of law for a brief time after the war, but the old ancestral tradition prevailed and he returned to the army to make his career. It was the period of the Wild West, and he played a full part in the excitement and action of the frontier. He spent seven years on the frontier, sometimes fighting, but often working for peace with the Indians as the railroads and cattlemen made their way west.

After his tour of duty in the West, Arthur MacArthur, now a captain in the regular army, was ordered to Jackson Barracks, located near New Orleans. It was here that he met and fell in love with Mary Pinkney Hardy, the daughter of a Virginia cotton merchant. They were married at the Hardy ancestral home near Norfolk.

The young Mrs. MacArthur had been gently and comfortably reared, but she quickly adapted to the rugged life of an army wife. Three sons were born—Arthur, then Malcolm, then Douglas—about two years apart. The first two were born at their mother's family home in Virginia, but Douglas entered the world on January 26, 1880, at the Arsenal Barracks in Little Rock, Arkansas, where his father was stationed—a fitting birthplace for one destined to serve his country across the globe.

There were thirty-eight states in the union at that time. Arkansas was one of them, but Little Rock was a long way from the pleasant, well-established life east of the Mississippi. Yet it was more settled than the wild Southwest, with its cattle kings, bandits, and warlike Apache Indians. The MacArthur family moved there a few months later when Captain MacArthur was transferred to Fort Wingate, New Mexico, in what was then the Arizona Territory.

Soldiers were needed to protect settlers against the raids of the fierce Apache Indians, led by their chiefs, Geronimo and Cochise. The Apaches planted gardens and then left them for long periods to go and hunt. When they returned, they often found white settlers who had moved in during their absence. The Indians retaliated with bloody raids on settlements and wagons. Stagecoach drivers were offered triple pay to take their passengers through the most dangerous Apache country, where they almost always encountered trouble.

Douglas MacArthur and his brother Arthur spent their first years at Fort Wingate, New Mexico. Soldiers were needed to protect settlers against the raids of the fierce Apache Indians, led by their chiefs, Geronimo (shown below) and Cochise.

When the MacArthur family left Little Rock they first had to make the long trek, hundreds of miles, to the Rio Grande. From there it took them eight long, hot days by covered wagon to get to Wingate.

Tragedy struck the family during their three-and-a-half year stay at Wingate. Malcolm, the middle son, died after a short illness. His body was brought back to Norfolk and buried in the Hardy family plot.

The surviving youngsters, Arthur and Douglas, spent their first years in a world filled with the sounds of pounding hooves, strident bugle calls, and distant Indian drums. They were seeing the last years of the untamed American frontier, for the country was developing rapidly and the world was changing at a faster than usual pace for this time in history.

Americans were building factories and the country was beginning to rival England as an industrial nation. Railroads were tying the country together and making industrial expansion easier.

Thomas Edison was working with a new wonder called the incandescent lamp. He was considering the problem of how to produce and transport enough electricity to light a city.

Henry Ford had left the family farm in Michigan and was repairing watches for a living while thinking about the automobile.

It was a time of empire building, and Great Britain led the way. Queen Victoria was at the height of her long reign, and men like Cecil Rhodes were making fortunes in African mining while extending the British Empire. Holland, Belgium, Portugal, Germany, and France also were carving empires in Africa. India was under British rule.

And all through this period, waves of immigration were adding population and strength to the United States, the great "Melting Pot of Democracy" which was fast becoming one of the great powers of the world.

When Douglas was only four years old, two years before Geronimo was captured, Captain MacArthur and his company were ordered to march overland 300 miles to Fort Selden. This fort was on a bend of the Rio Grande about 60 miles above El Paso, and was a better strategic spot from which to fight the Apache raiders. On the long, hot wagon trip, little Douglas trudged along the dusty way with the foot soldiers whenever his parents would allow it.

The squat, flat-roofed adobe buildings of Fort Selden overlooked the Rio Grande on one side and the desert on the other. There were only about sixty people in this small, lonely garrison in the heart of Apache country.

Douglas and Arthur played at being soldiers on the dusty parade ground. They learned to ride and shoot before they could read or write. They loved the outdoor life and learned to admire the courage and stamina of the soldiers they emulated.

There was no formal school available, so Mrs. MacArthur took on the task of educating her young sons. As Douglas later recalled, "Our teaching included not only the simple rudiments, but above all else, a sense of obligation. We were to do what was right no matter what the personal sacrifice might be. Our country was always to come first."

The young MacArthur boys were seeing the last years of the untamed American frontier. America was beginning to rival England as an industrial nation. Railroads were tying the country together and making industrial expansion easier. Steamboats were a common sight on American waterways.

In the evening, after the flag was lowered and darkness settled on the fort and cool air flowed in from the desert, they enjoyed storytelling time around the fire. Douglas and Arthur loved to hear their father tell stories of adventures on the frontier. He had known such colorful characters as Wild Bill Hickok and Buffalo Bill, as well as Indian scouts and gunslingers, and he told exciting tales about all of them.

Growing up in this military life, with a daily atmosphere of adventure, it never occurred to either Douglas or Arthur to follow any other careers. They were proud of their father's success and by the time they were teen-agers they both knew they wanted to become career officers.

Arthur, however, had a yearning for the sea and the distant places it could take a man. His goal was the Naval Academy at Annapolis, Maryland, and he won an appointment.

Douglas' goal was the Military Academy at West Point, New York, and Arthur's success at being admitted to Annapolis spurred him on to reach that goal. When his father was stationed at San Antonio, Douglas entered West Texas Military Academy and studied hard. He graduated first in his class with an extraordinary average of 97.33 per cent.

His father was now a lieutenant colonel stationed in St. Paul, Minnesota. Douglas and his mother spent a year in Milwaukee while he studied for his West Point entrance examination. He passed the test with a high grade, but had to wait another year for an opening at the academy.

In the meantime, the Spanish-American War had broken out and his father went to the Philippines as a brigadier general. It was with great pride that he read a letter from his wife with the news that Douglas had at last been admitted to West Point.

The ancestral tradition was continuing. The battle cry sounded again.

This illustration shows life at Fort Selden, where MacArthur spent several years of his childhood. The country around the fort abounded with colorful characters of the fast-disappearing American frontier.

West Point Cadet

Douglas MacArthur arrived at West Point in 1899, thrilled at the sight of the tradition-hallowed academy and eager to prove himself a worthy cadet. Since his father was serving in the Philippines, his mother moved to West Point with him and took up residence in a hotel near the academy. This immediately involved him in controversy. Upper classmen sneered that he was the first cadet in history to have his mother go through West Point with him. Douglas gritted his teeth and tried to ignore their remarks. His mother was a strong influence on his life, and his off-duty hours visits with her were a source of inspiration to him.

At that time, the practice of hazing first-year cadets was an established custom at West Point. Some of the upper classmen resented Douglas' calm, confident air, which they felt was arrogance. He was a

Douglas MacArthur arrived at West Point (left) in 1899, thrilled at the sight of the tradition-hallowed academy and eager to prove himself a worthy cadet.

MacArthur, pictured at the left, was a handsome, well-groomed young West Point cadet in 1903. The picture above shows his mother, Mary Pinkney Hardy MacArthur, as she appeared in 1900, when she lived near her son at West Point. Douglas' father, General Arthur MacArthur, is shown below.

handsome, well-groomed young man who always seemed to know exactly where he was going, and his self-pride was evident. First-year cadets were expected to submit to rough treatment in hazing, so the upper classmen wasted little time in giving Cadet MacArthur "the treatment."

It was known that his father was a general, and they continually reminded him of it. Many times at dinner, just as he was about to begin his meal, they would order him to stand and recite tales about his father's adventures in the Civil War. Finally, when his food was cold and everyone else had finished the main course, he would be allowed to sit down and eat.

One evening after the sun had set and the flag-lowering ceremony had been completed, he was ordered to report to a tent on the drill field occupied by six upper classmen who were waiting for him.

"Well, gentlemen, this *is* an occasion," the leader of the hazing group said sarcastically. "As you know, our distinguished visitor is the son of General Arthur MacArthur, and is guaranteed to be a hero himself someday."

The others bowed in mock reverence. Then the leader made scathing remarks about Douglas' mother being at West Point, called him a snob, a spoiled brat, and a show-off for having scored such a high mark on his entrance examination.

Cadet MacArthur's eyes flashed with anger, but he bit his lip and stood rigidly at attention. He was determined not to give them the satisfaction of seeing him lose his temper.

"Mister MacArthur, we don't like your posture," the leader said. "You have a choice of a calling-out fight with members of the boxing team, or accepting discipline."

Douglas knew the tradition of fighting members of the boxing team. If a plebe won, he had to continue fighting other members of the team until he was finally beaten himself. Thinking of his mother's shock if she learned about him indulging in beatings like this, he decided to accept the discipline.

"Start doing knee bends!" he was ordered. Holding his back straight in a military posture, he began the exercise. He was in rugged physical condition, and he kept performing the exercise over and over. Perspiration poured down his face as he continued on—longer than the upper classmen had seen other cadets last in this wearing test.

They watched in amazement as MacArthur continued the knee bends, straining every muscle to keep going. They did not give him the order to stop.

Finally, after a long period of time, Douglas collapsed and pitched forward on his face, unconscious. He was quickly revived with a pail of water thrown over him.

"You stopped before I told you to, mister!" the leader yelled. "Now start doing push-ups!"

Douglas shook his head to clear it, then wearily began a long series of push-ups. His aching arms trembled as he forced himself on and on, clenching his teeth. Then with a groan he fell unconscious again.

He was revived again, and the torture continued for another hour. The leader kept waiting for him to give in.

"Are you ready to beg for mercy, or are you still playing the hero, mister?" he taunted. Cadet MacArthur remained defiantly silent.

His tormentors finally gave up, and Douglas staggered back to his quarters and collapsed. A short time later his body was wracked with convulsions and he suffered severe abdominal cramps all through the night. His roommate and some of the other cadets were worried and wanted him to report to sick call in the morning, but he refused. He reported for duty as usual and somehow managed to get through the day without letting on that he was in pain.

When word got around among the cadets, Douglas won a new respect that he hadn't enjoyed before. The leader of the hazing group, frustrated because he hadn't been able to break the young cadet's iron will, admitted that the son of General MacArthur had more courage then he had thought.

"I'll say this," he remarked to Douglas, "you're no mama's boy!"

The cruelty of the hazing system was getting out of hand, and it led to tragedy two years later. A plebe who had been hazed unmercifully died shortly after leaving the academy. Public indignation mounted, and President McKinley ordered an investigation into the treatment of cadets at West Point.

The severity of Douglas' hazing was known, and he was summoned before the investigating committee and questioned. He was under oath and had to avoid giving false testimony, yet he refused to name his tormentors and incriminate them. The investigation led eventually to abolishing the hazing system.

Cadet MacArthur hated the senseless cruelty of it, and when he became an upper classman he refused to take part in any hazing.

Douglas studied tremendously hard, spurred on by his ambition to graduate with top grades in his class. He had some spirited competition from Ulysses S. Grant III, grandson of the great Civil War general and President of the United States. The two young men made no secret of their ambition, and were resented by some cadets.

Even in his West Point days MacArthur inspired fierce emotions, pro and con. His friends were extremely loyal and admired his talent. His enemies said he lacked modesty and was arrogant.

One cadet said, "To know MacArthur is to love him or hate him. You just can't like him!"

MacArthur, summoned before a committee investigating hazing at West Point, refused to name those who had tormented him as a cadet. The investigation led eventually to the abolishment of the hazing system.

There was little doubt about his absolute honesty, even though it was this trait that made some people dislike him. He refused to court popularity by disguising his ambition and being "just one of the boys." He had exceptional ability and he knew it. He had a habit of being bluntly truthful, no matter whose toes he stepped on, and he spoke out when he believed he was right, no matter what it cost him in popularity.

MacArthur once said, "My grandfather advised me, 'never talk more than is necessary.' Unhappily, I have not always emulated this lesson."

But diligent student that he was, Cadet MacArthur wasn't serious all the time. He was a good dancer, liked parties, and had an eye for pretty girls. He is remembered for a prank in which he and some friends raised the reveille cannon to the roof of his dormitory. Six strong men were required to bring it down off the roof the next day.

Some of his classmates claimed years later that Douglas had been engaged to eight girls at the same time, breaking the academy record of seven. When asked about it, he said with a twinkle in his eye, "I do not remember being so heavily engaged by the enemy."

When Graduation Day came on June 11, 1903, Douglas MacArthur was at the head of his class with an astounding four-year average of 98.14. He also held the highest student military rank of first captain. He was head of the student body and voted the cadet most likely to succeed.

Many years later when he had won almost every honor and medal possible for a military man, he still considered his graduation from West Point as the proudest event of his life.

"I can still say, that is my greatest honor," he said.

Now he was ready for the long road and the many trials and honors that lay ahead.

Pacific Duty

While Douglas MacArthur was attending West Point, his father had been involved in momentous events. The Spanish-American War had broken out in 1898 when the United States had gone to the aid of the people of Cuba, who were fighting for their independence from Spain. The Spanish rule of Cuba had been marked by cruelty and injustice. When the American battleship *Maine* was blown up in Havana Harbor, the United States had quickly declared war.

It was a short war and the Americans were easy victors. They quickly drove the Spanish forces out of Cuba, which led to that country's independence. A young adventurer named Theodore Roosevelt led a cavalry group know as the "Rough Riders" in a now-famous charge at San Juan Hill in one of the more exciting Cuban battles. His fame carried him to the Presidency of the United States a few years later.

Another area of the conflict was the Philippine Islands, which were also ruled by Spain. American forces sailed across the Pacific and attacked the main city of Manila by land and sea. The American fleet, under Admiral George Dewey, sailed boldly into Manila Bay with guns blazing and destroyed the Spanish fleet without losing a man.

While Douglas MacArthur was attending West Point, his father fought in the Philippine Islands during the Spanish-American War. Here, the American fleet, under Admiral George Dewey, sails boldly into Manila Bay with guns blazing, to destroy the Spanish fleet without losing a man.

After Spain's surrender, the Philippine Islands were ceded to the United States. Emilio Aguinaldo (above) formed an army to drive the Americans out of the country when he learned that the people were not to be given immediate self-government. The Filipinos were excellent guerrilla fighters, and the conflict raged for a long time in the remote jungle areas. At right, natives are pictured approaching a Philippine guerrilla camp. American troops under the command of General Arthur MacArthur finally captured Aguinaldo and the conflict soon ended.

A short while later, American and Filipino army forces attacked Manila. Brigadier General Arthur MacArthur was in command of the Second Brigade of the First Division, which performed brilliantly in some of the fiercest fighting. The Spanish defenders surrendered Manila and a treaty of peace was signed with Spain shortly afterward. Arthur MacArthur was promoted to major general.

Under the terms of the peace treaty, Spain ceded the Philippines to the United States. Many Americans felt that their country should not rule foreign lands as other imperialist countries did. But President William McKinley pointed out that the Spanish rulers had not prepared the Filipinos for self-government. There were few educated leaders to guide the small nation's future, and the economy was in trouble.

America's job was to prepare the Philippines for freedom and self-government, he said, and then eventually to set the country free. This announcement came as a shock to some of the Filipinos, who had expected self-government immediately after Spain surrendered. A tough, wily leader named Emilio Aguinaldo proclaimed himself leader of "the Revolutionary Government of the Philippines" and formed an army. He was determined to drive the Americans out of the country.

General Arthur MacArthur was in command of the American army, and his troops defeated the Filipino troops of Aguinaldo in a series of fierce battles. But the Filipinos were excellent guerrilla fighters and the conflict raged for a long time in the remote jungle areas. Finally MacArthur's troops captured Aguinaldo and brought him to Manila. MacArthur treated him kindly and placed him in custody almost as a guest in his official residence, Malacanan Palace. With their leader captured but treated generously, the rebellious Filipinos lost much of their desire for further fighting, and the conflict ended.

General Arthur MacArthur was
appointed Military Governor of the
Philippines, and he immediately
turned his efforts toward making
the country strong and democratic.
Much to the Filipinos' surprise, he
ordered the American army to set
up schools, build roads, and improve
harbors and ports. The cruel and
unjust Spanish system of law was
replaced by a modified system.
Filipinos came to respect and admire General MacArthur as a great
leader who was helping the country
and showing them a new and better
way of life.

Arthur MacArthur left the Philippines in 1902 and assumed command of the West Coast defenses of
the United States. When Douglas
finished West Point, he was on hand
to see his brilliant son graduate. It
was a proud day for the MacArthurs.
Their oldest son, Arthur, had graduated from the Naval Academy at
Annapolis a few years before and
had launched a successful career.
Now their youngest had made an excellent beginning. Soon the father
would be promoted to lieutenant general, becoming the highest-ranking
officer in the United States Army.

Douglas MacArthur could hardly
wait to begin his military career.
It was an exciting time for a young
officer to plan his future. The vigorous Theodore Roosevelt was now
President of the United States and
a spirit of enthusiasm prevailed.
The Wright Brothers made their
historic first flight the year Mac-
Arthur graduated, and Henry Ford
began making automobiles in De-
troit. American influence in the
world was growing.

As the top man in his graduating
class, Douglas MacArthur was allowed to choose the branch of the
army in which he wished to serve.
He chose the Corps of Engineers,
where advancements were more
rapid. Hero worship for his famous
father was natural in a young man
who hoped to follow in his foot-
steps, so it was no surprise that
Douglas MacArthur requested duty
in the Philippines.

When Douglas MacArthur graduated from West Point, he requested duty in the Philippines. When he arrived in Manila, he was assigned to the construction of barracks, roads, and wharves. The drawing above shows a pier under construction on an outlying jungle-covered island.

He soon arrived in Manila and was immediately assigned to the construction of barracks, roads, and wharves. The young second lieutenant was charmed by the lush tropical islands. As he put it years later, "The delightful hospitality, the respect and affection expressed for my father ... the languorous laze that seemed to glamorize even the most routine chores of life, the fun-loving men, the moonbeam delicacy of its lovely women, fastened me with a grip that has never relaxed."

MacArthur hadn't been there long when he received his baptism of fire. While constructing piers on an outlying, jungle-covered island, he marched a detachment of men into the forest to cut timber. The area was known to be infested with bandits. As MacArthur walked along a narrow jungle trail he was ambushed by two of them — one on each side of the trail.

There was a roar of gunfire and an enlisted man slumped to the ground. As MacArthur dropped to aid the man, a rifle bullet tore through the top of his campaign hat, splitting the small tree behind him. His frontier boyhood had made him an expert shot, and the young lieutenant took advantage of his experience. He whirled, drew his pistol, and dropped both bandits "dead in their tracks."

The foreman of the detachment, a grizzled sergeant, came rushing up. He looked at the dead bandits while chewing slowly on his quid of tobacco, then examined MacArthur's bullet-torn hat.

"Begging the lieutenant's pardon," he drawled, "but the rest of the lieutenant's life is pure velvet."

Douglas MacArthur returned to the United States for duty the following year, wearing the silver bar of a first lieutenant. The lure of the Pacific Islands was in his blood, and he hoped to return to that fascinating area of the world.

The opportunity came sooner than he had expected. Japan and Russia went to war with each other in 1905, fighting over territory in Manchuria. President Theodore Roosevelt was suspicious of Japan's aggressive plans to dominate the Far East. He wanted an expert military opinion of the Japanese army in action and ordered General Arthur MacArthur to act as chief American observer with the Japanese forces.

Lieutenant Douglas MacArthur was elated when he found he had been appointed his father's aide-de-camp. The assignment was extended to include a sweeping tour through the countries of the Orient, many of which were under colonial rule of European nations. General MacArthur was to report on the conditions in Japan, and to assess the temper of the people, the military forces and defenses, and the good and bad features of the colonial rule in each of the other countries.

It was a happy nine-month tour of duty for both father and son. They endlessly discussed politics, economics, and military facts.

Douglas related, "....We sat in the charmed circles of the chancelleries of the strong and the weak. Kings and viceroys and high commissioners lay bare their hopes and fears. . . . We saw the strengths and weakness of the colonial system, how it brought law and order, but failed to develop the masses along the essential lines of education and political economy. . . ."

The tour took the American observers to such exotic places as

".... We sat in the charmed circles of the chancelleries of the strong and the weak. Kings and viceroys and high commissioners lay bare their hopes and fears .... "

In 1905, Lieutenant Douglas MacArthur was appointed aide-de-camp to his father, General Arthur MacArthur, who had been ordered to act as chief American observer with the Japanese forces. The two spent a happy nine-month tour of duty in the countries of the Orient.

Hong Kong, Singapore, Rangoon; the Indian cities of Calcutta and Bombay; the countries of Siam and Indo-China, and China itself.

In Japan Douglas MacArthur was struck by the thrift, courtesy, friendliness, and charm of the ordinary Japanese people. They seem to appreciate the dignity of productivity and labor, and frowned on idleness and wastefulness. He was impressed with the devotion the people had for their emperor, who was not just a leader to his people, nor even a man, but a god. Yet the government of the country was not solely in the hands of the emperor. His government officials had a strong voice and the emperor depended on their advice.

The young MacArthur was worried because many of these government officials were members of the samurai, the traditional warrior aristocracy of Japan. Through their leadership Japan already had conquered Formosa, Korea, and Manchuria, and they were urging more conquest. These warriors had a religious belief in their destiny to make Japan master of Asia and the Pacific. MacArthur knew that this included the Philippines.

Douglas MacArthur returned to the United States with a knowledge of the Far East and a conviction that the destinies of Asia and the Western nations were interwoven— a conviction that today has been proven undeniably true.

South of the Border

Douglas MacArthur's education and experience as a professional soldier continued to grow as he took on a variety of challenging assignments. In 1906 he attended the Engineer School of Application at Washington. Shortly afterward he became aide-de-camp to President Theodore Roosevelt. This gave him an excellent opportunity to discuss international politics with the President and other civilian government officials, thus broadening his education.

The duties of a professional military man include many things besides fighting, although MacArthur did plenty of that before his long career was over.

As a graduate engineer he was sent to Wisconsin to work on river and harbor projects. From there he was sent to Fort Leavenworth, Kansas, to serve with the Third Battalion of Engineers. He had a company to train in bridge building and demolition and he turned an unlikely group into a team of experts. It was while he was on his tour of duty at Leavenworth that he requested and received permission to visit Panama, where the canal was under construction. Now, as a captain, he studied the huge engineering, supply, and sanitation problems in Panama.

By the time Captain MacArthur was back at Leavenworth there was trouble and tension along the Mexican border, and he was sent to San Antonio, Texas. No fighting materialized. While there, he enjoyed an opportunity to visit his old school, West Texas Military Academy. Soon after his return to Leavenworth, he was made head of the Department of Engineering at the Service Schools.

Douglas' father, General Arthur MacArthur, had returned from the Orient at retirement age in 1909 and had settled in the family home in Milwaukee. By 1912 he was in failing health, but he was cheered by a forthcoming reunion of his beloved Civil War regiment, the Twenty-fourth Wisconsin. The ninety veterans of the conflict still alive

in the regiment wanted their old comrade, who had since won so many honors, to attend. Arthur MacArthur was ill at this time, but though his doctor said he must not go and his wife pleaded with him not to go, the retired general was not to be deterred. He had a prominent role in the reunion program, and as he stood on the speakers' platform reminiscing about the Civil War days, he suddenly collapsed and died of a heart attack.

The adjutant took down the flag near the platform and draped it over the body of General Arthur MacArthur. As he did so, he himself collapsed, never to regain consciousness. This episode marked the dissolution of the regiment.

When the grief-stricken Douglas MacArthur was ordered back to Washington for duty, he took his widowed mother to live with him. His career received another boost shortly afterward when he was selected as a member of the General Staff at the unusually young age of thirty-two. He was personally chosen by the Army Chief of Staff, General Leonard Wood, because of reports that he had done an excellent job in his other assignments.

One thing General Wood especially liked about young Captain MacArthur was that he always stated his convictions, regardless of consequences. This trait became evident very soon, when MacArthur began filing minority reports on matters that were usually discussed by committees on the General Staff. Some of the senior officers on the staff resented young MacArthur giving his own opinions rather than going along with the majority. They resented it even more when they found out that General

As a captain, Douglas MacArthur requested permission to visit Panama, where the canal was under construction. By this time, he was a graduate engineer, and appreciated the opportunity to study the huge engineering, supply, and sanitation problems in Panama. The drawing at the left shows the canal locks under construction.

Wood liked the intelligent ideas MacArthur presented in his reports. Some of them harbored this resentment all during MacArthur's career, and continually tried to belittle his accomplishments in later years.

Trouble was stirring in many parts of the world while MacArthur was on the General Staff. General Victoriano Huerto had seized power in Mexico and was deliberately harassing Americans who did business in his country. In April, 1914, American forces closed the port of Veracruz, Mexico, where much of the trouble had occurred. Marines occupied the city.

Douglas MacArthur was ordered to Veracruz as an observer of the General Staff, "to obtain, through reconnaissance and other means . . . all possible information which would be of value in connection with possible operations."

When he arrived, MacArthur discovered that the occupying troops were having great difficulty in getting supplies into the city. Trains were necessary for this, but all the Mexican locomotives had disappeared.

The inquisitive captain from Washington was soon checking many information sources, and he found some vital information. Five Mexican locomotives lay hidden in a town about forty miles south of Veracruz. MacArthur didn't bother to inform the American military command, but made his way stealthily to the town and recruited some native railroad workers by offering them gold coin. He promised each one $150 if he would help him locate the engines. It would be no easy job, since they would have to get past Mexican soldiers and also bandits who might ambush them. The workers agreed.

Only three of the locomotives they found were usable; these were marked for use before MacArthur and the workers jumped on a handcar and set off down the track in the darkness of night. American troops would be able to seize the locomotives when MacAr-

thur pinpointed their location on a map. The task now was to get back to American lines safely.

The two workers pumped the handcar as MacArthur peered into the dank, foggy night. As they approached each town, the American captain would detour around it on foot while the Mexicans pumped the handcar through it. Then they would meet on the other side. On one of his detours, MacArthur ran into five bandits who began firing at him in the darkness. Drawing his automatic revolver from his holster, he shot from the hip and downed one of them, then managed to escape.

The handcar continued on through the night. It began to rain. At another town down the track MacArthur detoured around again and was groping his way through fog and darkness when he ran straight into a group of mounted Mexicans. He had startled them, and they began to yell and wheel their horses around, colliding with each other. Rifles were unslung and shots were fired in the darkness, but they couldn't see the lone American.

Three rifle bullets tore through MacArthur's uniform, but miraculously, he escaped a direct hit. One bullet grazed his hip, and another his ribs. He dove into some bushes and the bandits began firing at random into every bush they saw. Now MacArthur's western marksmanship came into play. Taking careful aim at silhouettes, he fired four shots and hit three bandits in a row. The others galloped off into the night. The weary American captain breathed a sigh of relief.

But the night was not over yet. A few miles farther on, as they were pumping along, they were attacked by horsemen who chased them.

"Faster!" MacArthur yelled to the workers on the handcar.

Pumping furiously, they managed to outdistance all the riders except one who had an unusually fast horse. Bullets blazed in the dark as he got closer and closer. Finally he was alongside the car, and a

bullet ripped through MacArthur's loose shirt, missing him. Then another caromed off the pumping handle an inch from his hand and a third plowed into the car close to his foot. MacArthur fired twice at close range, and the horse and rider went down violently.

At last they reached the final leg of the wild journey—a boat trip across a river. "We found the boat where we had left it," MacArthur recalled, "and started to cross the Jamapa River, but when near the shore the boat struck a snag in the darkness and sank. Fortunately the water at this point was less than five feet deep, for in our exhausted physical condition I do not believe we would have been capable of swimming.... Day was breaking when we reached the bank. We located another handcar and ran in close to Veracruz where we crossed the lines."

General Wood recommended MacArthur for the Congressional Medal of Honor for his bravery, but it was turned down by the War Department. However, he was promoted to major shortly afterward, and continued on the General Staff.

Even more trouble was brewing in Europe than in Mexico. Events were evolving into the great conflict that is known today as World War I.

The situation in Europe had become tense, explosive. Many things contributed to this condition, among them the unfriendliness of the neighboring countries of Austria and Serbia. Archduke Francis Ferdinand of Austria was assassinated by a Serbian and this was the spark that set off the conflagration.

Austria declared war on Serbia. Russia was friendly with Serbia and

In 1914, MacArthur was ordered to Mexico, where there had been trouble. One night he was fired at by a group of Mexicans on horseback. Taking careful aim, MacArthur fired four shots and hit three bandits in a row.

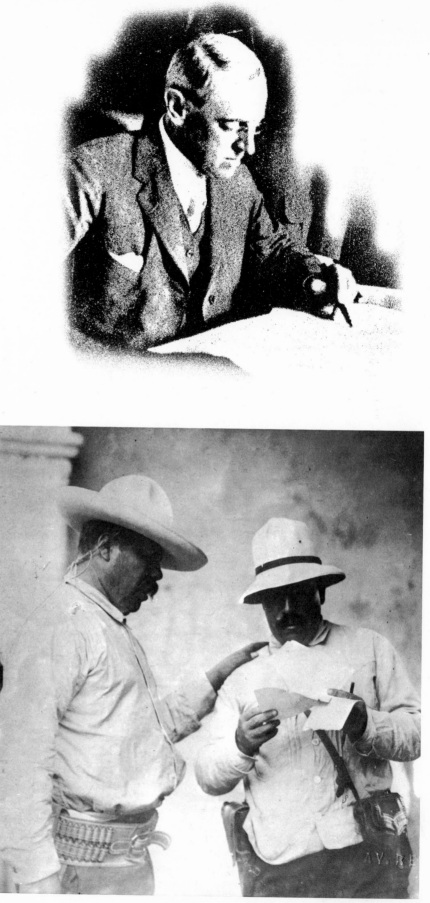

declared war on her enemy. Germany backed Austria. France went to the aid of Russia. Germany, caught between two great powers, overran little Belgium, disregarding all treaties, to try to knock out France before Russia could attack from the other direction. England went to the aid of France.

In 1916, the United States was still free of involvement in Europe, but was plagued by trouble on the Mexican border. One of the army's top generals, John J. Pershing, was sent to chase down and punish the outlaw Pancho Villa, who had been raiding along the border and up into the United States.

Woodrow Wilson was President. He was determined to keep the United States out of the war in Europe. Military leaders were warning of the need to prepare, however, and France was pleading for help. Things got worse when German submarines began sinking American ships in the Atlantic. Many American lives were lost; indignation mounted. Finally, on April 6, 1917, the United States declared war on Germany.

America, at peace for many years and isolated from the rest of the world by two oceans, had a relatively small army. Career officers like Douglas MacArthur knew that a big job of preparation lay ahead. Once again it was time for the American army to prove itself.

In 1916, General John J. Pershing (far left) was sent down to Mexico to chase and punish the outlaw Pancho Villa (bottom left), who had been raiding along the border and up into the United States. Even more trouble was brewing in Europe than in Mexico. Events were evolving into the great conflict that today is known as World War I. President Woodrow Wilson (top left) had been trying to keep the United States out of the war in Europe, but finally, in April, 1917, the United States declared war on Germany.

The sinking of the British liner, Lusitania (right), by a German submarine cost many American lives. This was one of the main occurrences that led the United States to enter World War I.

The Rainbow

No one knew better than Major Douglas MacArthur that it takes time to train and equip an effective wartime army. It would be many months before the small American army could be expanded to provide a huge fighting force for the war in Europe. In the meantime, America's allies, the French and British, were in need of help in their struggle against the hard-fighting German army.

MacArthur's position in Washington made it possible for him to discuss military matters with high-ranking government officials, including Secretary of War Newton D. Baker. MacArthur hit upon an idea that impressed the Secretary: why not activate units of the National Guard to provide troops for immediate European service? These trained men could fight while the army was training huge numbers of recently drafted citizens for later service at the front.

Secretary Baker brought Mac-Arthur to the White House one afternoon to discuss the idea with President Wilson. As they sat in the President's office, Secretary Baker explained that he would like to send one full division overseas, but that he faced a difficult decision. For example, if he selected the California National Guard, families of these men would feel it was unfair to send them first. Also, other states would protest that he was favoring California for the honor.

"There is a way out of the problem, Mr. Secretary," MacArthur said. "Why not choose units from many states and form one division? Then there could be no objections." He swung his arm in a half circle and declared, "This division would stretch from one end of the country to the other—like a rainbow!"

President Wilson thought for a moment and said, "That's exactly what we'll call it—the Rainbow Division."

MacArthur was assigned to the new division as chief of staff under its commander, the aging General William Mann. General Mann gave him a virtually free hand, and Mac-Arthur plunged into the business of training the division at Camp Mills, New York. In August, 1917, he was promoted to infantry colonel. By December he had landed in France with the new division, ready for action.

World War I was unlike previous wars, because of technological progress. Automobiles and trucks were in general use, but long-distance overland transportation for troops was by railroad boxcars labeled "8 horses or 40 men." Still, much of the time soldiers moved on foot through the mud and slush.

The British had developed the armored tank, which began to rumble its threatening way into combat. The first flimsy two-seater airplanes appeared in the sky. They were used for observation, for bombing, and for firing machine guns at ground troops. Soon they were fighting each other in air battles. Ace pilots such as the German Baron von Richtofen

World War I was unlike previous wars, because of technological progress. The British had developed the armored tank, and the first flimsy two-seater airplanes appeared in the sky. They were used for observation, for bombing, and for firing machine guns at ground troops. Ace pilots such as the German Baron von Richtofen (above) and the American Captain Eddie Rickenbacker (right) became heroes.

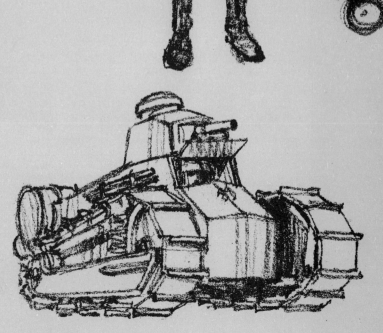

and the American Captain Eddie Rickenbacker became heroes.

Before the Rainbow Division was forced to face the test of making an attack, MacArthur had been awarded his first Silver Star medal for "extraordinary heroism and gallantry in action." He had risked his life to join a small French raiding party going after German prisoners. They had been forced to fight their way back, and MacArthur had fought harder than anybody.

Finally the Rainbow Division swung into action in a fierce battle. MacArthur led his men out of the trenches "over the top" in a direct attack on the German lines.

He remarked, "You never know about men until a time like that. You never know what's inside them. I thought I knew what was inside our men, but after all, they were not really professionals. None of them had ever been under fire.

"And then, there we were—ready to go. When the time arrived, I climbed out and started forward. For a dozen terrible seconds, as I went forward, I felt that they weren't following me. But then, without turning around, I knew how wrong I was to doubt even for an instant. In a moment, they were all around me . . . ahead of me."

For eighty-two days in a row the Rainbow Division took part in intense front-line fighting. Colonel MacArthur insisted on leading attacks, even though some officers back at headquarters considered this an unecessary risk for a leader of his rank. A general told him, "You have no business leading attacks like some expendable line officer!"

"General," MacArthur replied, "I don't consider line officers in the Rainbow any more expendable than I am. I lead them to prove it, and I believe it promotes a fighting spirit."

MacArthur's feats were becoming legendary. His courage and daring under fire were matched by his colorful appearance. He refused to wear a steel helmet in battle, but instead wore a battered officer's cap. He wore immaculate riding breeches and mirror-polished boots in the trenches, along with a four-foot long muffler knitted by his mother. "The Beau Brummel of the American Army" and "The Fighting Dude" he was called, but his men loved it. "He can chase Germans as well as any doughboy in the Rainbow," said one proudly. But many officers at headquarters considered MacArthur a show-off and resented the attention he was getting.

In the spring and early summer of 1918, the Germans concentrated all their strength in a great push toward Paris. The Communist Party had taken over Russia in a revolution and signed a peace treaty with Germany. Now the Germans could move all their forces to France, and they were anxious to score a victory before huge numbers of American troops poured into France. The American army was now built up. Twenty-nine divisions—more than

The photos at the right show action in France during World War I. In December, 1917, Douglas MacArthur, now an infantry colonel, had arrived in France with the Rainbow Division under his command.

a million men—were sent to France to join the Rainbow Division in the fighting. The Germans fought their way to within fifty miles of Paris before they were stopped at Château-Thierry.

Marshal Foch, the Supreme Commander of Allied Forces, now decided it was time for a counter attack. The Rainbow Division attacked from the west side of the town of Château-Thierry and the French army from the east side. The Germans withdrew, and the Rainbow Division was ordered to pursue them. This proved to be a fierce operation. The Germans had not just pulled back, they had dug into the hills and set up small units in the woods. There were six days of bitter fighting. Finally MacArthur, by employing Indian tactics and sending out small groups of scattered units to knock out gun emplacements with grenades, managed to break the German resistance. The Rainbow Division, with half its men killed or injured, moved on to Sergy, a village that had changed hands many times. The retreating

Germans were pressed so that they could not make a stand until they reached the Vesle River.

By this time, MacArthur had earned his fourth Silver Star. The division was given a rest and a chance to build up with replacements. MacArthur was promoted to brigadier general in recognition of his achievements.

The offensive against St. Mihiel, south of Verdun, was wholly an American operation. The Americans hit the German line and pushed right through, gaining considerable territory. MacArthur had a fifth Silver Star.

The Allied offensive drive continued on to the eighty-mile front of the Meuse-Argonne section near the German border. An intense, bitter battle raged at Côte de Chatillon and MacArthur and the Rainbow Division were in the thick of it. Although casualties were extremely high, the stronghold finally fell. The Germans knew now that they faced total defeat in the war.

The war ended on November 11, 1918, when an armistice was signed.

In the photo above, General John J. Pershing pins the Distinguished Service Cross on Brigadier General Douglas MacArthur for leading the Eighty-fourth Brigade, Forty-second Rainbow Division at Château-Thierry, France, September 7, 1918. MacArthur received two wound stripes, twelve other decorations, and seven other citations in World War I.

The medals shown below, from left to right, are the Silver Star, the Distinguished Service Medal, the Legion of Honor (a French medal), and the Distinguished Service Cross.

In October, 1918, the Rainbow Division took part in the last great offensive of the war on the Meuse-Argonne front. A million American troops hurled themselves against the German Hindenburg Line.

One of the key points in the enemy defense was a heavily fortified hill called Côte de Chatillon. It's defenders had resisted all attacks and had slowed the entire American advance in that sector. The rainy fall weather had turned the battle landscape into a soggy quagmire of mud.

Young Brigadier General Douglas MacArthur received his orders: the Rainbow Division would take Côte de Chatillon, no matter what the cost. It would be no easy task. The hill was surrounded by barbed wire. Behind the wire lay machine guns and artillery, poised to annihilate attackers as they tried to cut their way through. A direct frontal attack would mean tremendous casualties. MacArthur ordered aerial reconnaissance maps to be made of the hill. A few hours later, as he studied them, he discovered a small gap in the barbed wire on one flank.

That night he led a brigade of men through the opening in the wire, crawling through the cold, wet mud. They carried bayonets and knives as they crept silently through the dark toward the German gun positions. The defenders of the hill expected a daylight attack in full scale; they had not considered the possibility of a silent night raid. Many of the gunners and guards had relaxed.

MacArthur and his men spread out to cover all the enemy trenches and gun pits. Then they leaped into them, bayonets flashing. The attack was so well timed that resistance soon collapsed.

Advancing American troops were astonished the next morning to see the Stars and Stripes and the regimental colors of the Rainbow Division flying atop Côte de Chatillon. Officers were even more astonished to find that an important victory had been won with very few casualties. Douglas MacArthur had proven that intelligent military strategy saves lives.

Thirty-eight-year-old Douglas MacArthur left Europe as the youngest division commander of the war. He had received two minor wounds and been gassed once. He had also won nearly every medal the American and French armies could bestow, including the Croix de Guerre, two Distinguished Service Crosses, and seven Silver Stars.

His Rainbow Division fame earned him a key postwar assignment: superintendent of West Point. In the words of General Peyton March, Chief of Staff, MacArthur's job would be to "bring the academy up to date, modernize the course of study, outlaw hazing, and reorganize the whole institution."

During the war, the four-year course at West Point had been cut to one year in order to meet the pressing need for officers. Much of the fine old spirit of the academy was gone and the curriculum was outdated.

The job was a staggering one, but MacArthur plunged into it with his usual enthusiasm. He brought his mother to live with him in the superintendent's residence. He worked long hours and did an amazing job of overhauling the academy.

One of the things he stressed most was an improved English course. When one instructor protested that English was not important, he replied, "We are not training military weapons here — we are training military *minds*. Without a solid grounding in English, no officer can grasp or communicate the subtleties and complexities of international conflicts in the twentieth century. The pen, sir, is *still* mightier than the sword!"

MacArthur was a man who appreciated the value of both the pen and the sword. He was proficient with each of them. After three years of wielding the pen at West Point, he longed for a more active assignment and he got it. Orders came for his transfer back to the Philippines. The call of the islands sounded again for him; he packed his bags with enthusiasm.

"....The pen, sir, is still mightier than the sword!"

The scenes at the right were taken at the United States Military Academy at West Point, New York, where MacArthur became superintendent when he returned from duty in Europe after World War I. The photo on the left at the top of the page shows the Administration Building, where the office of the superintendent is located. At the top of the page on the right is the cadet chapel, and the photo at the bottom of the page shows cadets in review in the Central Area parade ground.

Bataan and Corregidor

Douglas MacArthur stood on the deck of the transport *Thomas* as it steamed into Manila Harbor. The channel ran between the high bluff of the Bataan Peninsula and the island of Corregidor, jutting out of the water three miles away. It's good to be back, he thought, for he already felt a strong kinship with the Filipino people from his father's ties there and from his own previous tour of duty.

It had been eighteen years since his previous tour. Now his life had changed, and he had a wife with him. In typical MacArthur fashion, he had swept a charming socialite named Louise Brooks off her feet and married her suddenly. But the marriage was destined not to last; they were to be divorced several years later.

He was pleased to see the Philippines making steady progress toward the day when they would be independent. The economy had improved and there were fine new roads, hospitals, schools, and buildings everywhere. A distinguished Filipino leader, Manuel Quezon, was president of the Philippine Senate and one day would become the country's first president. He and MacArthur became close friends.

They both realized that Japan was becoming more powerful and aggressive, and that the Philippines stood in the path of any Japanese conquest in Southeast Asia. Japan would someday want to capture the Philippines as a base for military operations against the other Asian countries and Pacific islands.

MacArthur's most important task was to draw up defense plans. With the small Filipino and American forces deployed there, he knew it would be hopeless to defeat a large Japanese army, but they could delay it until fresh troops arrived.

The best place to do this would be the rugged Bataan Peninsula, covered with bamboo thickets, jungle, and mountains. He spent weeks roaming the whole area, planning defensive maneuvers and familiarizing himself with every square mile of it. He also examined the rock-like Corregidor Island, off the end of the peninsula. It was a natural fortress with its caves and perfect places for gun placements.

MacArthur's tour of duty was a short one, but he was later to return to the Philippines for another period of duty. Between the tours in the islands he was promoted to the highest job in the United States Army—chief of staff—where he served five years. MacArthur argued constantly for more Congressional appropriations for defense forces, but the United States was in the midst of a depression and his requests were turned down by an economy-minded Congress. Trouble was again brewing in Europe where Adolf Hitler was gaining power, organizing an army, and threatening war. Japan had become even more aggressive in Asia and had invaded China.

After three years at West Point, MacArthur was transferred back to the Philippines—eighteen years after his previous tour of duty there. He became a good friend of Manuel Quezon (shown in the drawing at the top of page 58), who would later become the Philippine's first president.

The illustration at the bottom of page 58 shows Chinese refugees from the 1931 Japanese invasion of China. At about this same time, trouble was brewing again in Europe, where Adolf Hitler was gaining power, organizing an army, and threatening war.

MacArthur continued to be a controversial figure during his tenure as chief of staff. Older officers whom he had bypassed on the way to the top job envied him and criticized his actions. The country was in an economic depression and World War I veterans who needed money felt they were entitled to an immediate bonus for their service. Many of the original 17,000 staged a march on Washington and for two months camped in tents and packing crates in the city. Feelings were heated and the mob became riotous after being incited by Communists who were taking advantage of the political unrest caused by the widespread unemployment in the country.

The Secretary of War decided that the District of Columbia could not handle the situation and asked for help from President Hoover, who ordered Chief of Staff MacArthur to disperse the mob, using force

if necessary. Assisted by his aide, Major Dwight D. Eisenhower, who was destined to become a famed general and President of the United States, MacArthur commanded the troops who forced the crowd of bonus marchers out of the city. No shots were fired in this unpopular action, but MacArthur was criticized in the newspapers—one cartoon pictured him riding a white horse while directing action against the "ragtag" marchers.

MacArthur's last peacetime tour of duty in the Philippines had come about when the islands became a commonwealth. MacArthur was sent as military adviser to the Philippine Commonwealth.

The United States agreed that after ten years of this status, the Philippines would become an independent nation. Manuel Quezon, who became President of the Philippine Commonwealth, asked his old friend MacArthur if the islands

The picture on page 60 shows General Douglas MacArthur taking oath of office as chief of staff with rank of four-star general, on November 12, 1930.

In the picture above, a detachment of World War I veterans who had marched on the Capitol at Washington, D.C. in July, 1932, in quest of a bonus are shown as they begin to leave the city. General MacArthur commanded the troops who forced the bonus marchers out of the city. Below left, one bonus-seeking veteran, still fighting, is carried off to jail. General MacArthur (below right) takes a break while in charge of cleaning bonus marchers' camps in Washington.

would be defensible against attack.

"Yes, with ten years' time and much help from the United States," he replied.

MacArthur remained on active duty as military adviser to the Philippine Commonwealth until he felt compelled to retire to give himself the independence from Washington necessary to accomplish his job. He became a field marshal in the Philippine Armed Forces and prepared to set up the island's defenses.

Tragedy struck twice for Douglas MacArthur during his tours of duty in the Philippines. He received word in Manila that his brother Arthur, who had become a captain in the Navy, had died of appendicitis. Then, on his last peacetime tour in the islands in 1936, his elderly mother died while living there with him. She had been a strong influence in his life, and his grief was overwhelming. "Of the four of us who had started from the plains of New Mexico," he said, "three were now gone, leaving me in my loneliness only a memory of the households we had shared, so filled with graciousness and old-fashioned living."

A happy period in his life began when he met and fell in love with a lovely young woman from Tennessee named Jean Marie Faircloth. A year and a half later, in 1937, they were married. "It was perhaps the smartest thing I have ever done," he remarked years later. "She has been my constant friend, sweetheart, and devoted supporter ever since. How she has managed to put with my eccentricities and crotchets all these years is quite beyond my comprehension."

In February, 1938, a son was born to the MacArthurs in Manila. There was little hesitation before they named the baby Arthur, in honor of his grandfather and uncle. He was the latest in a long line of Arthur MacArthurs stretching back to the hills of Scotland.

Douglas MacArthur and Manuel Quezon worked hard to build a citizens' army in the Philippines. MacArthur spent long evenings in his study, poring over military books and maps. But they were not to have the necessary ten years to complete the Commonwealth's defenses.

Funds were short, and though MacArthur pleaded for more aid, Congress was reluctant to authorize much money for the defense of the Philippines. State Department officials agreed with Congress.

Their attention was focused on Europe, where tension had built to the breaking point again, two decades after World War I. Adolf Hitler had built a tremendous military force in Germany. In September, 1939, he unleashed this force on the Allied countries of Poland, France, and England. The neutral nations of Belgium and the Netherlands were conquered by German troops because they lay in the path toward France. This time the Germans were not to be denied in France. Their modern military equipment, well-disciplined troops, and great numbers of warplanes swept them to victory over the French and English defenders. France surrendered and the British forces had to retreat to England, which was bombed daily by the powerful German air force. The United States remained neutral, but gave military aid to Great Britain. The British refused to

Shown at right is Mrs. Douglas MacArthur, the former Jean Marie Faircloth.

"....How she has managed to put up with my eccentricities and crotchets all these years is quite beyond my comprehension."

surrender, and Germany suddenly invaded Russia, inflicting great casualties on that country.

Meanwhile, the United States demanded that Japanese forces get out of China and stop trying to dominate Asia. Tension grew between the two countries until the military leaders in Japan decided to go to war to achieve their aims. They felt that if they could destroy the United Stated Pacific fleet in a lightning blow and seize control of the Philippines, the Dutch East Indies, and other Asian lands rich in natural resources, the United States would be forced to let them have their way.

On July 27, 1941, General MacArthur was recalled to active duty and was assigned to command the United States Army Forces in the Far East. All Filipino forces were integrated into the American armed forces.

On the morning of December 7, 1941, Japanese warplanes attacked without warning the United States fleet at Pearl Harbor in Hawaii and inflicted great damage. They succeeded in destroying many ships, crippling America's naval forces in the Pacific.

When MacArthur heard the news over the radio in Manila, he knew what was in store for the Philippines. He regretted that he hadn't had time to complete the ten-year defense program for the islands, and that the United States hadn't sent more aid. There were only 12,000 American troops under his command, and 120,000 Filipino Citizen National Army soldiers. They had little artillery, few tanks, and outmoded weapons. The whole air force in the Philippines had fewer than a hundred airplanes.

MacArthur didn't have to wait long for the blow to come. The next day, huge numbers of Japanese bombers struck, destroying many of the American planes. A short while later, more than 200,000 well-armed Japanese troops invaded the Philippines and advanced toward Manila. They had overwhelming

The picture at the top of page 65 shows a view of Pearl Harbor, Hawaii, on the morning of December 7, 1941, as Japanese warplanes attacked the United States fleet stationed there. The picture at the bottom of the page shows the capsized U.S.S. Oklahoma and the U.S.S. Maryland after the attack.

numbers of tanks, artillery, and ammunition.

MacArthur's plan was to set up a resistance that would slow the Japanese advance until fresh supplies and troops could be shipped into the Philippines by the United States. The plan was doomed, however, by the success of the Japanese attack at Pearl Harbor. Because the war in Europe had priority, the American navy wasn't permitted to use ships to keep the supply lines open to the Philippines. Soon MacArthur's meager supplies of food, ammunition, and fuel were running low.

The outnumbered Filipino and American troops fought gallantly and slowed the Japanese drive. MacArthur's brilliant strategy frustrated the enemy. Their main object was to capture the capital city of Manila and Manila Bay, where they could ship supplies to be used in their Asian campaigns. They landed two large forces from different directions, planning to trap MacArthur's troops between them on the broad, flat plain around Manila. MacArthur, however, skillfully evacuated his troops to the rugged highlands of the Bataan Peninsula while fighting a rearguard action. He declared Manila an open city, leaving it undefended so the enemy would not have to bomb it. At first the Japanese military leaders were elated. They had captured Manila, and MacArthur was cornered on the peninsula. Then they realized that capturing Manila did them no good at all, for they could not use it as a supply port. MacArthur's carefully hoarded artillery on Bataan and Corregidor would blast their ships out of the water if they tried to enter the harbor. The discouraged enemy realized that he would have to fight a long, hard battle to drive MacArthur out before he could use the port of Manila. "The enemy might have the bottle," MacArthur said, "but I have the cork."

MacArthur's men fought stubbornly for every inch of ground on the rain-soaked, muddy hills of Bataan. Their leader made his headquarters on Corregidor, taking his wife and young son with him.

Though MacArthur had left Manila undefended in December, 1941, the Japanese bombed the city (above right) when they realized that capturing it did them no good. They could not use Manila as a supply port, for if they tried to enter the water, MacArthur's artillery on Bataan and Corregidor would blast their ships out of the water. Below right: Japanese troops advance on Manila, January 3, 1942.

The Japanese knew he was there, and bombed the island unmercifully, until there was hardly a tree or building standing on the whole island. For three months the MacArthurs made their home in the underground network of tunnels that comprised his headquarters, living with the crash of bombs and artillery shells around the clock. Little Arthur celebrated his fourth birthday there. Mrs. MacArthur insisted on staying with her husband.

The policy in Washington was that the war in Europe had priority; that the Philippines would have to be expendable. MacArthur's requests for aid brought no results. But the heroism of his men inspired everyone in America and gave the nation hope at a point in the war when America was losing battle after battle. His gallant stand made Filipinos and other Asians realize that America would fight for them, and this stiffened their resistance. It threw off the whole Japanese timetable of conquest.

On Corregidor, MacArthur walked around amid bombs and shells without a steel helmet, encouraging his men and directing the defense. Some critics have argued that it was unnecessary for a general to risk his life in such a manner, but MacArthur felt strongly that it was an important part of leadership.

"It was my duty to my men," he said. "When the soldiers saw me, they would say, "I guess if the Old Man can take it, I can, too."

In the spring of 1942, it was evident that MacArthur could not maintain his position much longer. The frustrated Japanese were pouring all their might into taking Bataan and the island of Corregidor. President Franklin Delano Roosevelt ordered MacArthur to leave the Philippines and go to Australia to assume command of all United States forces in the Southwest Pacific. MacArthur protested, but the order was final.

The President said, "I know that every man and woman in the United States admires with me General MacArthur's determination to fight to the finish with his men in the Philippines. But I also know that every man and woman is in agreement that all important decisions must be made with a view toward the successful termination of the war. Knowing this, I am sure that every American, if faced individually with the question as to where General MacArthur could best serve his country, would come to only one answer."

MacArthur's friend and second-in-command, General Jonathan Wainwright, was left in command of the meager forces in the Philippines.

Hasty secret plans were made for getting MacArthur to Australia. The general would take his wife and son and a few members of his staff on this hair-raising journey. To get to Australia they would have to slip away under cover of darkness and run the gauntlet of the Japanese navy. The odds were not promising.

MacArthur decided to put his faith in the speedy motor torpedo boats, known as "PT boats," for the first leg of the perilous journey, despite strong opposition from some advisers who urged that submarines be used.

Shortly after the sun plunged into the western sea on March 11, 1942, MacArthur and his little group boarded the small boats. He said goodbye to his grimy, battered troops and shook hands with General Wainwright. "We're all alone, Jonathan," he said. "Washington

isn't going to send reinforcements. If I get through to Australia, you know I'll come back. In the meantime, you've got to hold." There were tears in his eyes when he turned away.

The four PT boats, led by Navy Lieutenant John Bulkeley, started off into the darkness, threading their way through mine fields. During the night the boats separated, going singly to the appointed secret rendezvous. The small boats offered little protection from the rough sea, and everyone was drenched with spray.

Only one boat arrived at the rendezvous by dawn. The others, including MacArthur's, had to continue in broad daylight, easy prey for any alert Japanese ship or plane. They spent four more harrowing days and nights escaping Japanese detection before boarding two American B-17 airplanes to fly to Australia.

A determined MacArthur arrived in Australia. When reporters asked him for a statement, he said grimly, "The President of the United States ordered me to break through Japanese lines. . . . I came through and I shall return."

The prophetic statement echoed around the world. It inspired Americans, cheered the people of the Philippines, and it served notice on the enemy that this determined commander refused to accept defeat.

For three months the MacArthurs, including young Arthur, made their home in the underground network of tunnels that comprised his headquarters on the island of Corregidor. They lived with the crash of bombs and artillery shells around the clock. Arthur (above left) celebrated his fourth birthday there. The picture at the left shows the officers quarters on Corregidor after it took a beating from Japanese bombs.

"I Shall Return"

The year 1942 was a grim one in Australia, where General Douglas MacArthur coordinated the American, Australian, and New Zealand military plans. Bataan and Corregidor had fallen and the surviving troops were treated brutally by their captors. They were forced to march many miles in exhausting heat to prisoner-of-war camps. They were weak from malaria and lack of food, and as they stumbled along, enemy guards beat them unmercifully. Thousands died along the route, and the event came to be known as "The Bataan Death March." MacArthur swore to avenge these tragic heroes.

With the Philippines captured at last, the Japanese were able to speed up their plans to conquer the other countries of the Far East. Hong Kong, Singapore, Malaya, Burma, Indo-China, and the Dutch East Indies had felt the onslaught of Japanese military might. The sparsely populated nation of Australia lay in the path of the enemy,

and it seemed only a matter of time before the Japanese would occupy sufficient bases on the island of New Guinea to launch an invasion.

MacArthur's immediate task was to stop the Japanese drive. His constant requests to Washington gradually resulted in the sending of more troops and supplies. He began to build up a sizable armed force of soldiers, sailors, marines, and airmen. In the meantime, he frustrated enemy attempts to build up troops and supplies at New Guinea bases designed as jumping-off points for Australia. His small naval forces and aviation groups fought bravely against larger enemy forces, destroying Japanese shipping again and again. Several enemy task forces were smashed and driven back.

The Japanese rallied on the northeastern coast of New Guinea, out of range of MacArthur's Australian-based bombers, and launched an overland attack. They climbed the 10,000-foot Owen Stanley moun-

In 1942, Bataan and Corregidor fell. The Japanese now planned to conquer the other countries of the Far East. They wanted to use the island of New Guinea to launch an invasion on Australia, which lay in their path. MacArthur frustrated Japanese attempts to build up troops and supplies at New Guinea bases. The photo above shows a raid by Air Force bombers on Japanese shipping and shore installations on the island. At right, a Japanese fuel dump goes up in flames after a direct hit by U.S. destroyers. Navy PT boats like the one below were based in inlets and river mouths on New Guinea. They participated in the campaign that won the Japanese base at Lae. PT boats slipped out for sudden night attacks that earned them the name "Green Dragons" from the Japanese.

tain range and bore down toward Port Moresby, an ideal invasion-launching site only 350 miles from Australia.

MacArthur moved with lightning speed, air-ferrying troops and supplies to Port Moresby to meet the Japanese. He stopped them only thirty-three miles from Moresby, chased them back over the mountains and took two of their vital positions, Buna and Gona. Now the tide was beginning to turn.

MacArthur's forces swept up the northeastern coast of New Guinea, taking Japanese-held Salamaua and Lae. He established footholds in western New Britain and the northern Solomons, and seized the Admiralty Islands. The Japanese continued to reel back, stung and often perplexed by MacArthur's battle methods.

MacArthur had a passionate belief that men's lives should be spared whenever possible, and that direct frontal assaults on enemy strongholds resulted in unnecessary loss of lives. He wanted to save as many young American and Australian men for postwar life as he could. This philosophy motivated him to develop his unique strategy of bypassing strong Japanese centers and hitting seemingly less important positions. It was called "leap-frogging" and it worked.

Years later a Japanese colonel explained how: "This was the type of strategy we hated most. The Americans attacked and seized, with minimum losses, a relatively weak area, constructed air fields and then proceeded to cut the supply lines to our troops. Our strong bases were gradually starved out because we could get no supplies through to them. The Japanese army preferred direct assault after the German fashion, but the Americans flowed into our weaker points and submerged us, just as water seeks the weakest entry to sink a ship." MacArthur's forces lost fewer lives in his whole Pacific campaign than the Americans lost in one single battle at Anzio Beach

In the photo above, Yank infantrymen proudly display a Japanese flag taken from enemy headquarters in New Guinea. In the photo at the top of page 73, General MacArthur pushes through New Guinea jungles in a jeep, inspecting the forces that would soon chase the Japanese back from Port Moresby and over the Owen Stanley mountain range from which they had come. The picture at the bottom of page 73 shows Australian infantrymen firing at Japanese soldiers during the final assault that took the vital position of Buna, New Guinea.

in Italy, when they stormed ashore against heavily fortified German defenses.

As his forces advanced closer and closer to the Philippines, a dominant theme kept running through MacArthur's mind: "I shall return!" At last American troops invaded the islands after fierce naval and air battles, and Japanese resistance gradually crumbled. Joyous Filipino guerrilla fighters, who had harassed the Japanese conquerors for two and a half years, helped round up prisoners and shoot it out with die-hards who refused to surrender.

In October, 1944, a landing barge thundered ashore on the island of Leyte, in the Philippines. It struck bottom fifteen yards from shore and the gate clanked open. Into the water strode the erect figure of General Douglas MacArthur, wearing his familiar old gold-braided cap with the "scrambled eggs" leaf designs on it, and his dark glasses. There was no mistaking his identity. The defender of the Philippines had kept his pledge and was returning. Japanese snipers were still shooting in the vicinity, but this mattered little to the happy Filipinos, who welcomed MacArthur as they had welcomed no one else in their history.

"I have returned," he told them. "By the grace of Almighty God our forces stand again on Philippine soil ... soil consecrated in the blood of our two peoples. We have come dedicated and committed to the task of destroying every vestige of enemy control over your daily lives, and of restoring...the liberties of your people."

The war now was drawing toward a victorious end for the Allied countries. British and American troops had liberated France, wrested Italy from the Germans, and set Belgium and the Netherlands

In the photo at right, a landing barge has thundered ashore on the island of Leyte in the Philippines on October 24, 1944. When the gate clanked open, into the water strode General Douglas MacArthur. The defender of the Philippines had kept his pledge to return. Below, American troops bring in supplies to support invading forces on Leyte in November. By January, the United States Thirteenth Army Air Force carried out an initial raid (above) on a Japanese base on the island of Corregidor in Manila Bay. Within a month, most of the enemy forces had been driven from Manila and Luzon.

"....I have returned....By the grace
of Almighty God our forces stand again
on Philippine soil ...soil consecrated
in the blood of our two peoples...."

free. The Russians had defeated the Germans in eastern Europe, and Germany was now being invaded by all the Allied armies.

In other Pacific action, forces under Admiral Chester W. Nimitz had taken a number of island military bases from the Japanese. Finally, Okinawa and Iwo Jima were captured in fighting that cost thousands of American lives, and preparations to invade Japan itself were begun. American B-29's bombed the country day after day.

The Allies wanted to avoid a costly invasion if possible, and tried to persuade the Japanese to surrender unconditionally. The terms of surrender were not accepted, however, and it was finally decided to drop the newly-developed atomic bomb on two Japanese cities. This terrible weapon made the military rulers of Japan realize that further resistance was futile. Japan surrendered on August 14, 1945.

President Roosevelt had died a few months before, and his successor, Harry S. Truman, had immediately appointed Douglas MacArthur as Supreme Commander for the Allied Powers. The famed war hero, who had won the Congressional Medal of Honor for his gallant defense of Bataan and Corregidor, was now a General of the Army, wearing five stars on his uniform. His new job would be to direct the occupation of Japan.

MacArthur immediately made plans to fly to Japan. The members of his staff were worried about his setting foot in the homeland of a people who had considered him their bitter enemy for five years. More than two million Japanese soldiers were roaming the country, despite the fact that their government had surrendered, and there were no American troops there yet. Some of them could be expected to be bitter, and some might try to assassinate the enemy leader.

MacArthur felt strongly that the trip was a necessary gamble. He was familiar with Oriental psychol-ogy and was convinced that to earn the respect of the Japanese he should make a fearless appearance immediately.

A few days later his military transport plane, the *Bataan*, landed at Atsugi Airport. Members of his staff alighted, and then, as everyone stared, the figure of MacArthur emerged from the plane. He wore his customary open-necked shirt, sunglasses, and battered, goldbraided cap, and he carried his familiar long-stemmed corncob pipe. He looked around, climbed into a car and headed into Yokohama to set up details of the formal surrender and occupation.

Prime Minister Winston Churchill of Great Britain remarked, "Of all the amazing deeds of bravery of the war, I regard General MacArthur's personal landing at Atsugi as the bravest of the lot."

Soon after his arrival, MacArthur learned that General Jonathan Wainwright, whom he had left to defend Corregidor, was being released from a Japanese prisoner of war camp nearby. The two old friends had an emotional reunion. Wainwright was thin and sickly, and walked with a cane. MacArthur threw his arms around him, and both were so overcome with emotion that they couldn't speak for a couple of minutes. MacArthur insisted that Wainwright be his guest of honor at the surrender ceremony, to be held in Tokyo Bay.

The giant battleship *Missouri* was selected as the site of the formal surrender. At nine o'clock in the morning on September 2, 1945, the Japanese government officials stood on the deck of the *Missouri* and faced the representatives of the Allied Powers. Military men of all the countries lined the ship to witness the ceremony.

A table stood in the center of the deck, with the surrender document on it. MacArthur, as Supreme Commander, led the proceedings. He stepped to a microphone and faced the Japanese officials.

General of the Army
Douglas MacArthur steps
from his military trans-
port plane, the Bataan,
at Atsugi Airport near
Tokyo, Japan. From here
he went to Yokohama to
set up details of the
formal surrender and
occupation of the country.

"We are gathered here, representatives of the major warring powers," he began, "to conclude a solemn agreement whereby peace may be restored. . . . It is my earnest hope and indeed the hope of all mankind that from this solemn occasion a better world shall emerge out of the blood and carnage of the past—a world founded upon faith and understanding—a world dedicated to the dignity of man and the fulfillment of his most cherished wish—for freedom, tolerance and justice. . . . I now invite the representatives of the Emperor of Japan and the Japanese Government and the Japanese Imperial Staff Headquarters to sign the instrument of surrender at the places indicated."

After the representatives of all the countries had signed, Douglas MacArthur spoke briefly by radio to the people of the United States. Millions listened as his clear voice intoned solemnly: "Today the guns are silent. A great tragedy has ended. A great victory has been won. . . .And in reporting this to you, the people, I speak for the thousands of silent lips, forever stilled among the jungles and the beaches and in the deep waters of the Pacific which marked the way. . . ."

With mixed feelings of joy, pride, sadness, and hope for the future, the fighting general left the *Missouri* and went into Tokyo to begin his new duties. A milestone in American history had been reached.

General MacArthur signs the Japanese surrender papers aboard the U.S.S. Missouri *in Tokyo Bay as Lieutenant General Jonathan Wainwright (center) and Lieutenant General A.E. Percival (next to Wainright) watch the ceremonies. Both men had been prisoners of the Japanese.*

The Old Soldier

Douglas MacArthur did not look upon the job of directing the occupation of Japan as merely that of keeping the former enemy under his heel. He had a sense of history, and he felt that in the long run, Japan must be put back on her feet as a free and democratic nation, to take its rightful place in the world. This would require sweeping reforms and a new way of life to replace the old feudal, militaristic system.

The people had never had a choice in running their own lives. Ten powerful family clans, called Zaibatsu families, owned ninety per cent of the country's industries and refused to allow competitive free enterprise. They also forbade workers to have unions, and kept them in virtual serfdom. Women were not allowed to vote. The government of the country was tightly controlled by a few industrial and military leaders. Farmers who were virtually slaves, eked out a bare living on land owned by large estate owners.

It would be a tremendous feat to change all this. First, it would be necessary to establish the Supreme Commander's complete authority. The country lay in ruins, and there was widespread unemployment and food shortages. MacArthur knew he had to win the respect of the Japanese, and to do this, he had to be a remote, authoritarian figure, never mixing with crowds as an American politician might. This was the only type of leader they would respect at this point in their history. He also wanted to show them that he would be kind and generous, so he immediately began importing food from America to ease the shortage.

MacArthur adhered to a rigid, seven-day work week. He was almost never seen outside his residence at the American Embassy, except on his daily trips by limousine to his office in a large downtown building. Crowds gathered every day to watch him arrive for work and depart for home, much as they might watch royalty in other countries.

This restricted the MacArthurs' social life, but Mrs. MacArthur accepted it as absolutely necessary. Each morning the general would arise at seven, enjoy breakfast with his wife and son, then work at his residence until ten thirty. Then a limousine with his five star insignia would take him to his office. He would return home for lunch at about one thirty, then return to his office at four o'clock, where he sometimes worked until ten or eleven in the evening. The MacArthurs' main relaxation was watching movies shown at the residence. The general loved to watch western films, and this passion was shared by Mrs. MacArthur and Arthur.

MacArthur often entertained visitors from America, including his former aide, General Eisenhower, who paid a visit in 1946, when he was chief of staff in Washington. Many Congressmen called.

MacArthur was an avid reader. This wide reading and knowledge of world affairs constantly amazed his visitors, both official and non-official.

The Allied Council for Japan, consisting of representatives of the other Allied countries, was supposed to advise MacArthur on the occupation, but MacArthur was convinced he knew the right way to govern the country. He seldom sought or accepted their advice. This course of action upset the Russians, particularly, since they wanted to thwart some of his plans to make Japan a democratic country.

MacArthur's reforms were truly sweeping. He gave women the right to vote. He taxed the previously tax-exempt Zaibatsu industries and encouraged competition in industry. He gave workers the right to form unions and bargain for better conditions. He called a special Japanese committee and insisted that they form a constitution that guaranteed

The photo above shows Emperor Hirohito of Japan as he appeared in September of 1945. In the picture below, MacArthur opens the first session of the Allied Council for Japan on April 5, 1946. The council consisted of representatives of the other Allied countries and was organized to advise MacArthur on the occupation.

to the people civil rights such as freedom of speech, assembly, press, and religion. He set up local elections and insisted on an elected Japanese government. He freed the farmers by having the government buy the large estates they were working on and selling the land to them as small farms with twenty-five-year mortgages.

In five years MacArthur accomplished a democratic revolution in Japan, and the country has since become the most prosperous, modern, and free nation in all of Asia. Coming in as a military conqueror, he might have been remembered as a tyrant. But the Japanese people think of him today as a revered and beloved peacetime leader.

By 1950 the old soldier was seventy years old, and he began to think about going home to America to retire. He wanted Arthur to see his native country for the first time, and he wanted to relax and visit with old friends in his retirement. He was sure that his fighting days were over.

He was mistaken, however, for destiny called him to one last battlefield — on the peninsula called Korea. This country, which bordered on Communist China, had been held by Japan prior to World War II. At the end of the war, United States troops occupied the southern half and Russian troops the northern. Since no agreement could be reached for unifying the country, two separate governments were formed.

In the south, the Republic of Korea had been established after an election in 1948 that was supervised by a United Nations commission. In the north, the Russians refused to allow voting and established a Communist government. This government was aggressive and believed it could conquer the south and make the whole country Communist. In June, 1950, the North Korean armies invaded the Republic of Korea and quickly overran much of the country.

The United Nations Security Council voted to help South Korea

In June, 1950, the United Nations Security Council voted to help South Korea resist the invasion of the North Korean Communists. In this session, President Truman was asked to name a Supreme Commander for the United Nations forces that would take part in the conflict. He quickly named General Douglas MacArthur.

resist the invasion by force. A unified command was formed. Since the United States would have to supply most of the troops, President Truman was asked to name a Supreme Commander. He quickly named General of the Army Douglas MacArthur.

Once again the old soldier started out in battle without sufficient troops or supplies. Most of the limited number of American occupation troops in Japan were not experienced in battle, but they were the only men available until America could send more. MacArthur deployed them in a defensive position around the supply port of Pusan, to hold on until fresh troops and supplies could be sent. This was the only corner of South Korea not overrun by the invading Communists. MacArthur's men hung on grimly until help came.

Then came the turning point. With a brilliant stroke of strategy, MacArthur invaded at Inchon, far behind enemy lines, at a place where the enemy never expected him. In a series of lightning moves, the United Nations troops liberated Seoul, the capital city of South Korea, and cut off the invaders' supply lines. The Communists were thoroughly routed and chased back into North Korea. MacArthur didn't stop, but pursued them northward until U.N. troops had overrun most of North Korea. His familiar figure was seen inspecting battle positions everywhere.

It was at this point that Communist China entered the war with masses of troops and pushed the United Nations forces back into South Korea. MacArthur's forces rallied and again forced the Red armies back, and then the war became a stalemate. The U.N. forces could defeat the Communists by using the mighty air power of America to bomb their supply bases, but for diplomatic reasons MacArthur was denied permission. His bitter protests touched off the famous controversy that resulted in his dismissal by President Truman,

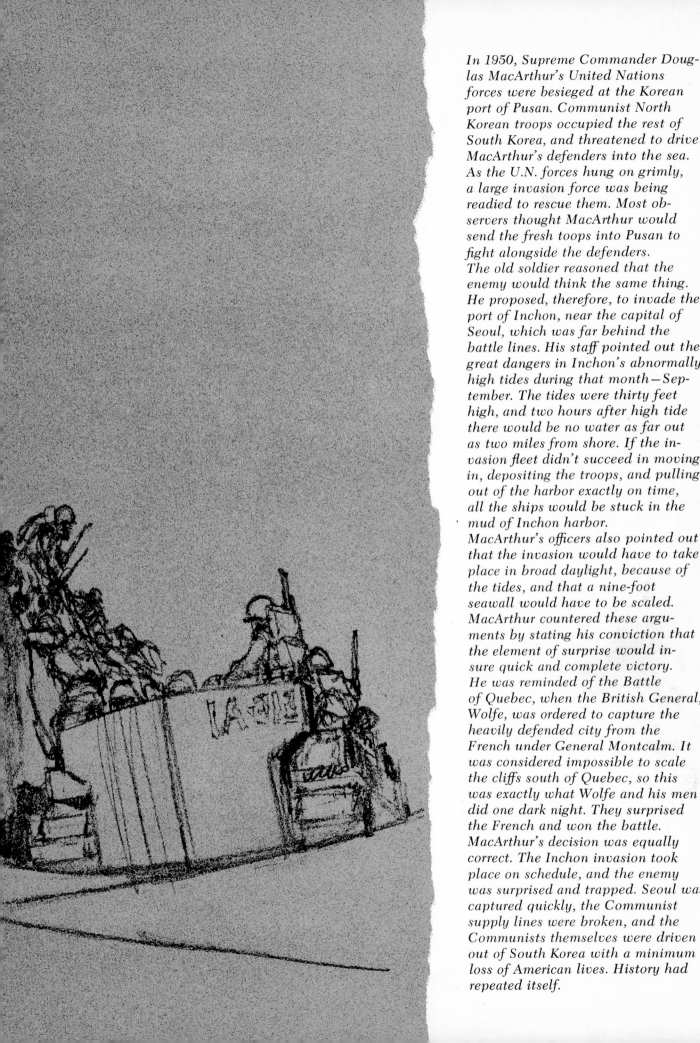

In 1950, Supreme Commander Douglas MacArthur's United Nations forces were besieged at the Korean port of Pusan. Communist North Korean troops occupied the rest of South Korea, and threatened to drive MacArthur's defenders into the sea. As the U.N. forces hung on grimly, a large invasion force was being readied to rescue them. Most observers thought MacArthur would send the fresh toops into Pusan to fight alongside the defenders.

The old soldier reasoned that the enemy would think the same thing. He proposed, therefore, to invade the port of Inchon, near the capital of Seoul, which was far behind the battle lines. His staff pointed out the great dangers in Inchon's abnormally high tides during that month — September. The tides were thirty feet high, and two hours after high tide there would be no water as far out as two miles from shore. If the invasion fleet didn't succeed in moving in, depositing the troops, and pulling out of the harbor exactly on time, all the ships would be stuck in the mud of Inchon harbor.

MacArthur's officers also pointed out that the invasion would have to take place in broad daylight, because of the tides, and that a nine-foot seawall would have to be scaled. MacArthur countered these arguments by stating his conviction that the element of surprise would insure quick and complete victory.

He was reminded of the Battle of Quebec, when the British General, Wolfe, was ordered to capture the heavily defended city from the French under General Montcalm. It was considered impossible to scale the cliffs south of Quebec, so this was exactly what Wolfe and his men did one dark night. They surprised the French and won the battle.

MacArthur's decision was equally correct. The Inchon invasion took place on schedule, and the enemy was surprised and trapped. Seoul was captured quickly, the Communist supply lines were broken, and the Communists themselves were driven out of South Korea with a minimum loss of American lives. History had repeated itself.

and the old soldier went home to be welcomed as a hero by the American people.

At last MacArthur could retire, but he did not fade from the national scene. He took up residence at the Waldorf Astoria in New York, and he delighted in showing the growing Arthur the many facets of life in America. Distinguished statesmen, military leaders, and prominent people from all walks of life paid him visits for many years afterward.

In 1952, MacArthur became Chairman of the Board of Remington Rand, Inc., a position he held until he died.

Despite his running battles with Congress over the years when he was demanding more military aid, the members knew that Douglas MacArthur fought only for what he felt was right for his country. When he was eighty-two years old, both houses of Congress unanimously passed a special resolution expressing the "thanks and appreciation of the Congress and the American people" for his outstanding leadership and devotion to his country. He thanked them and pointed out that a general was only as good as the troops he led. And he added proudly, "Mine were great!"

In 1961, the defender of the Philippines was invited to take a sentimental journey back to the land he loved and where he was revered. The government declared a national holiday when he landed, and the outpouring of love by the people of the Philippines moved him to tears.

A year earlier, Japan had awarded him the highest medal it could confer on a foreigner who was not a head of state, the Insignia of the Grand Cordon of the Order of the Rising Sun with Paulownia Flowers.

When the MacArthurs returned to the United States, they took up residence at the Waldorf Astoria in New York. The General delighted in showing his son the many facets of life in America. The family attended many sports events, and the General and his wife enjoyed theater visits and dances.

MacArthur lived to his last days in comparative happiness at his New York suite, with his beloved Jean and Arthur, who grew to be a handsome young man and a good student at Columbia University.

When he died in 1964, the nation mourned and his memorial rites were the object of world attention. His body lay in state in the Capitol in Washington as thousands of people filed past. He was entombed at the MacArthur Memorial in Norfolk, Virginia, the city of his mother's birth, in a building that was presented by that city. It is a handsome old courthouse in the center of the city, and it has been remodeled into a striking memorial hall. Visitors from all over the world come to visit the memorial, a great many of them from the Republic of the Philippines. Several rooms in the memorial contain the mementoes of the general's career, including his medals, presents from foreign countries, papers, battle flags, office furniture, and the black limousine that he used in Tokyo. But the most inspiring sight to visitors is a glass case in which have been placed his famed old cap, sunglasses, and corncob pipe. They are the instantly recognized symbols of a great American who placed honor, duty, and love of his country ahead of every other value during his life.

The name Douglas MacArthur is destined never to die. It can be heard every day in the Republic of the Philippines, when the roll is called at military bases. His name is carried on the rolls, and a sergeant responds, "Present in spirit!"

Douglas MacArthur will be "present in spirit" as long as patriotism plays a vital role in American life.

The photo above shows the widow of Douglas MacArthur shortly after his death in 1964. Opposite, the body of General MacArthur, borne upon a horse-drawn caisson, moves away from the Capitol on April 9 on its way to National Airport and burial at Norfolk, Virginia. Following the caisson is the general's personal five-star flag and farther in the rear is the riderless horse, symbolic of a fallen military commander.

"I shall return!" That ringing declaration, made in the gloom of seeming defeat, marked General Douglas MacArthur's destiny to succeed and triumph. It served notice on the enemy that America would not surrender, and it inspired the Asian people under Japanese military rule to believe that America would honor its pledge to liberate them.

MacArthur's background and character prepared him for the role he was to play in this historic crisis. A soldier of courage, dedication, and unshakable determination, he had proven many times before that he was equal to the challenge before him in this, his moment in history. He moved unfalteringly toward his goal, liberating the Philippines amid the cheers of a grateful people, and finally standing in triumph on the deck of the battleship *Missouri* as he accepted the enemy's surrender before the eyes of the world.

Douglas MacArthur personified the best of America to millions of people in other countries. His determination and courage, and the fairness and generosity he showed as military ruler of a conquered Japan, symbolized the essential decency and rightness of his country. These qualities sustained him and shaped his destiny as a towering figure in the pages of world history.

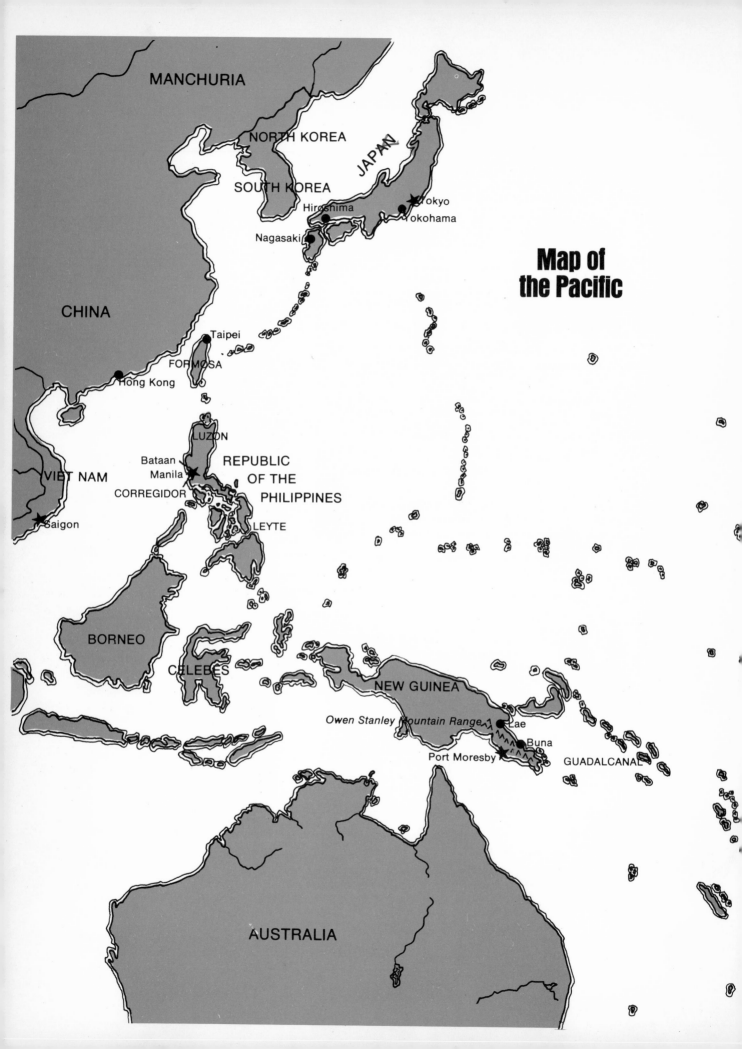

Map of the Pacific

MANCHURIA

NORTH KOREA

SOUTH KOREA

JAPAN

Hiroshima

Nagasaki

Tokyo

Yokohama

CHINA

Taipei

FORMOSA

Hong Kong

LUZON

Bataan

Manila

CORREGIDOR

REPUBLIC
OF THE
PHILIPPINES

VIET NAM

Saigon

LEYTE

BORNEO

CELEBES

NEW GUINEA

Owen Stanley Mountain Range

Lae

Buna

Port Moresby

GUADALCANAL

AUSTRALIA

Bibliography

ARCHER, JULES. *Front Line General; Douglas MacArthur.* New York: Julian Messner, 1963.

ARMY TIMES, eds. *The Banners and the Glory, the Story of Douglas MacArthur.* New York: Putnam, 1965.

BURNS, MARTIN. *MacArthur; the real story.* New York: Universal Publishing and Distributing Corp., 1951.

CONSODINE, ROBERT. *MacArthur the Magnificent.* Philadelphia: David McKay Co., 1942.

———. *General Douglas MacArthur.* Greenwich, Conn: Fawcett Gold Medal Books, 1964.

COUGHLIN, WILLIAM JAMES. *Conquered Press: The MacArthur Era in Japanese Journalism.* Palo Alto: Pacific Press, 1952.

EYRE, JAMES KLINE. *The Roosevelt-MacArthur Conflict.* Chambersburg, Pa.: Craft Press, 1950.

GANOE, WILLIAM A. *MacArthur Closeup; much then and some now.* New York: Vantage Press, 1962.

GORDON, ROSALIE M. *The MacArthur-Korea Story.* New Rochelle, N.Y.: America's Future, Inc., 1961.

GUNTHER, JOHN. *The Riddle of MacArthur.* New York: Harper, 1951.

HELMAN, FLORENCE, ed. *List of references in periodicals on Douglas MacArthur.* Washington: Library of Congress, 1942.

HERSEY, JOHN. *Men on Bataan.* New York: Knopf, 1943.

HIGGINS, TRUMBULL. *Korea and the Fall of MacArthur.* New York: Oxford University Press, 1960.

HUFF, SIDNEY L. *My Fifteen Years With General MacArthur.* New York: Paperback Library, 1964.

HUNT, FRAZIER. *MacArthur and the War Against Japan.* New York: Scribner, 1944.

———. *The Untold Story of Douglas MacArthur.* New York: Devin-Adair, 1954.

JENNINGS, C. WISE. *The MacArthur Saga, a poem.* Cloverdale, Va.: The author, 1951. (available at the N.Y. Public Library)

*JULIAN, ALLEN P. *MacArthur, the Life of a General.* New York: Duell, Sloan & Pearce, 1963.

KELLEY, FRANK R. *MacArthur Man of Action.* Garden City, N.Y.: Doubleday, 1950.

KELLEY, WILLIAM A. *MacArthur, Hero of Destiny.* Greenwich, Conn.: Fawcett Publications, 1942.

KENNY, GEORGE CHURCHILL. *The MacArthur I Know.* New York: Duell, Sloan & Pearce, 1951.

LEE, CLARK GOULD. *Douglas MacArthur.* New York: Holt, 1962.

*LONG, LAURA. *Douglas MacArthur, Young Protector.* Indianapolis: Bobbs Merrill, 1965.

MACARTHUR, DOUGLAS. *Let Us Remember-address to Rainbow Division 7/14/35.* Maysville, Ohio: Rainbow Division Veterans Assoc, 1942.

———. *MacArthur On War.* New York: Duell, Sloan & Pearce, 1942.

**———. *A Pictorial History of the Korean War.* Kansas City: V.F.W. memorial edition, 1951. (available at N.Y. Public Library)

———. *Address to Congress 4/19/51.* Chicago: Rand McNally, 1951.

———. *Revitalizing a Nation, opinions and beliefs.* Chicago: Heritage Foundation, distributed by Garden City (N.Y.) Books, 1952.

———. *Duty, Honor, Country; 2 addresses.* New York: Rolton House, 1962.

**———. *Duty, Honor, Country; a pictorial autobiography.* New York: McGraw-Hill, 1965.

———. *A Soldier Speaks; public papers and speeches.* New York: Praeger, 1965.

MACARTHUR, DOUGLAS. *Representative speeches, compiled by the Legislative Reference Service of the Library of Congress.* Washington: U.S. Govt. Printing Office, 1964, Senate Document #95.

———. *Reminiscences.* New York: McGraw-Hill, 1964.

MILLER, FRANCIS T. *General Douglas MacArthur, Soldier-Statesman.* Philadelphia: J.C. Winston, 1951.

———. *General Douglas MacArthur, Fights For Freedom.* Philadelphia: John C. Winston, 1942.

MUGGAH, MARY GATES. *The MacArthur Story.* Chippewa Falls, Wisconsin: The Chippewa Falls Book Agency, 1945.

NEWLON, CLARKE. *The Fighting Douglas MacArthur.* New York: Dodd-Mead, 1965.

NICOLAY, HELEN. *MacArthur of Bataan.* New York: D. Appleton, 1942.

PACIS, VINCENTE ALBANO. *National Defense in the Philippines.* Manila: Philippine Education Co., 1937.

PEARL, JACK. *General Douglas MacArthur.* Derby, Conn.: Monarch Books, 1961.

ROVERE, RICHARD. *The General and the President.* New York: Farrar, Straus & Young, 1951.

———. *The MacArthur Controversy and American Foreign Policy.* New York, Farrar, Straus and Giroux, 1965.

**SCHOOR, GENE. *General Douglas MacArthur, a pictorial biography.* New York: R. Field and Co., 1951.

SEBALD, WILLIAM JOSEPH. *With MacArthur in Japan.* New York: Norton, 1965.

STEINBERG, ALFRED. *Douglas MacArthur.* New York: Putnam, 1961.

SPANIER, JOHN W. *The Truman-MacArthur Controversy and the Korean War.* Cambridge, Mass.: Belknap Press, 1959.

U.S. CONGRESS, SENATE COMMITTEE ON ARMED SERVICES. *Hearings on MacArthur's dismissal by President Trumen.* Washington: U.S. Govt. Printing Office, 1951, Senate document #69.

WALDROP, FRANK C., ed. *MacArthur on War.* New York: Duell, Sloan & Pearce, 1942.

WILLOUGHBY, CHARLES A. *MacArthur, 1941-51.* New York: McGraw-Hill, 1954.

WHITNEY, COURTNEY. *MacArthur, his rendezvous with history.* New York: Knopf, 1956.

* Juvenile
**Pictorial

Index